Dad,
I Want to Hear
Your Story

A Father's
Guided Journal
To Share His Life &
His Love

Jeffrey Mason

DEDICATION

To Tommie Louis Mason
My Dad

You will always be my first example, my forever
mentor, the man I will always follow.

We are so alike in temperament
and the same in spirit. The lesson of your life
was to live and love with all I am,
never give up and always find a way.

Most cherished of all,
you taught me to love who I am
and always believe in what is possible.

Thank you for your love, your life, your example,
and your passion
for what can be.

I Love You Dad.

Dear goodness, I miss you.

"Listen,
there is no way any true man
is going to let children live around him
in his home
and not discipline and teach,
fight and mold them
until they know all he knows.
His goal is to
make them better than he is."
— Victor Devlin

"A child looks up
at the stars
and wonders.
A great father puts a child
on his shoulders
and helps them to grab a star."
— Reed Markham

"Every child grows up thinking their father is a hero or villain until they are old enough to realize that he is just a man"
— Mark Maish

"To all the loving, caring, supportive, protective, responsible fathers out there.
May God give more years to see your children flourish.
— DJ Kyos

IT'S YOUR BIRTHDAY!

"Fathering is not something perfect men do, but something that perfects the man." — Frank Pittman

1. What is your birthdate?

   _____

2. What was your full name at birth?

   _____

3. Were you named after a relative or someone else of significance?

   _____

   _____

4. In what city were you born?

   _____

5. Were you born in a hospital? If not, where?

   _____

6. What were your first words?

   _____

7. How old were your parents when you were born?

   _____

   _____

IT'S YOUR BIRTHDAY!
"Any man can be a father, but it takes someone
special to be a Dad." — Anne Geddes

8. What was your height (length) and weight at birth?

_____

9. Were you the oldest, middle, or youngest child? How
many siblings do you have?

_____

_____

10. What have your parents told you about how you were
as a baby?

_____

_____

_____

_____

_____

_____

_____

_____

_____

_____

IT'S YOUR BIRTHDAY!
"My father's love existed through his actions."
— Author Unknown

11. What stories have you been told about the day you were born?

_____

_____

_____

_____

_____

_____

_____

_____

_____

_____

_____

_____

_____

_____

_____

_____

_____

IT'S YOUR BIRTHDAY!

"We worry about what a child will become tomorrow, yet we forget that he is someone today." — Stacia Tauscher

12. What is your earliest childhood memory?

_____

_____

_____

_____

_____

_____

_____

_____

_____

_____

_____

_____

_____

_____

_____

_____

_____

FAMILY TREE

"The ancestor of every action is a thought."
— Ralph Waldo Emmerson

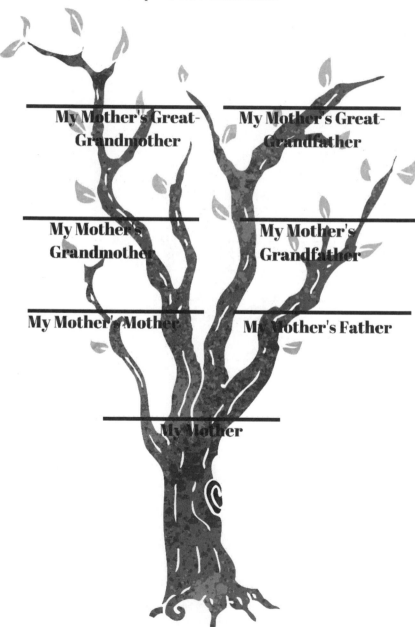

My Mother's Great-Grandmother

My Mother's Great-Grandfather

My Mother's Grandmother

My Mother's Grandfather

My Mother's Mother

My Mother's Father

My Mother

FAMILY TREE
"Each of us is tomorrow's ancestors."
— Unknown

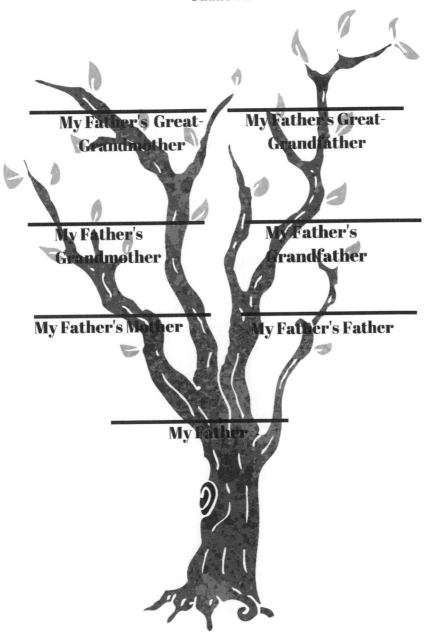

My Father's Great-Grandmother

My Father's Great-Grandfather

My Father's Grandmother

My Father's Grandfather

My Father's Mother

My Father's Father

My Father

GROWING UP

"By the time a man realizes that maybe his father was right, he usually has a son who thinks he's wrong."
— Charles Wadsworth

1. Where did you live in your elementary school years?

   _____

   _____

2. Did you have a nickname?

   _____

3. What was your favorite treat when you were a kid?

   _____

   _____

4. What were your regular chores?

   _____

   _____

   _____

   _____

5. Did you get an allowance? If yes, how much?

   _____

   _____

GROWING UP

"It is easier for a father to have children than for children to have a real father." — Pope John XXIII

6. Who was your best friend?

_____

_____

7. What did you do on a typical Saturday when you were a kid?

_____

_____

_____

_____

_____

8. What do you miss most about being a kid?

_____

_____

_____

_____

_____

_____

_____

GROWING UP

"Even though you're growing up, you should never
stop having fun." — Nina Dobrev

9. Describe what you were like when you were a kid.

_____

_____

_____

_____

_____

_____

_____

10. What was the worst trouble you remember getting
    into as a kid?

_____

_____

_____

_____

_____

_____

_____

WHERE HAVE YOU LIVED?

"Anyone can live in a house, but homes are created
with patience, time and love." — Jane Green

List the cities you have lived in during your life.
Include the dates if you can remember them.

_____

_____

_____

_____

_____

_____

_____

_____

_____

_____

_____

_____

_____

_____

_____

_____

THE TEENAGE YEARS

"Of all the titles I have been privileged to have, 'Dad' has always been the best." — Ken Norton

1. How did you dress and style your hair during your teens? Do you have any pictures?

   _____

   _____

   _____

   _____

2. Did you hang out with a group of people or a few close friends? Do you still talk to any of them?

   _____

   _____

   _____

   _____

3. In what kind of car did you learn to drive?

   _____

   _____

   _____

4. Who taught you to drive?

   _____

   _____

THE TEENAGE YEARS

"Few things are more satisfying than seeing your children have teenagers of their own." — Doug Larson

5. Did you date in high school? Did you have any serious relationships in your teen years?

_____

_____

_____

6. Did you have a curfew?

_____

7. Did you ever get in trouble for missing your curfew? What was your punishment?

_____

_____

_____

8. Did you go to any school dances? What were they like?

_____

_____

_____

_____

THE TEENAGE YEARS
"Little children, headache; big children, heartache."
— Italian Proverb

9. What was a common weekend night like during your teens?

_____

_____

_____

_____

_____

10. Knowing all you know now, what advice would you give your teenage self?

_____

_____

_____

_____

_____

_____

_____

_____

_____

_____

THE TEENAGE YEARS

"Having a teenager can cause parents to wonder about each other's heredity." — Unknown

11. Describe what you were like during your teen years.

_____

_____

_____

_____

_____

_____

_____

12. Write about a favorite memory from your teens.

_____

_____

_____

_____

_____

_____

_____

_____

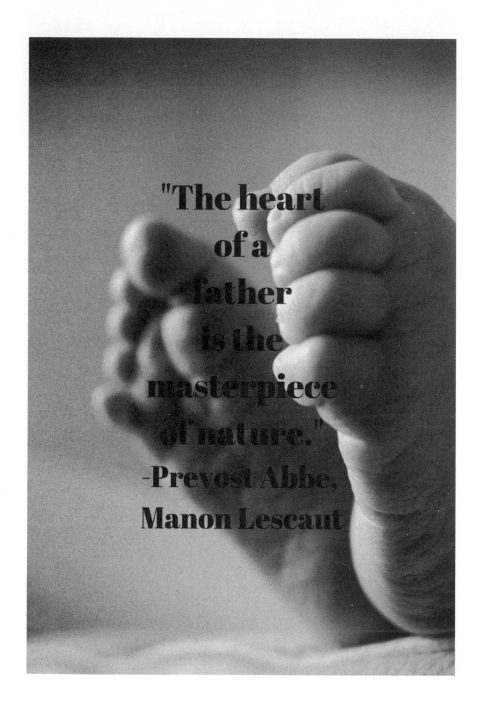

"The heart of a father is the masterpiece of nature."
-Prevost Abbe, Manon Lescaut

"Every man, if he takes time out of his busy life to reflect upon his fatherhood, can learn ways to become an even better dad."
- Jack Baker

WHAT HAPPENED THE YEAR YOU WERE BORN?

"My father didn't tell me how to live. He lived and let me watch him do it." — Clarence Budington Kelland

Google the following for the year you were born:

1. What historical events occurred?

_____

_____

_____

_____

2. What movie won the Academy Award for Best Picture? Who won for Best Actor and Best Actress?

_____

_____

_____

3. What were a few popular movies that came out the year you were born?

_____

_____

_____

_____

_____

WHAT HAPPENED THE YEAR YOU WERE BORN?

"The most important thing in the world is
family and love." — John Wooden

4. What song was on the top of the Billboard charts?

   _____

5. Who was the President of the United States?

   _____

6. What were a few popular television shows?

   _____

   _____

   _____

7. What were the prices for the following items?

   - A loaf of bread:
   - A gallon of milk:
   - A cup of coffee:
   - A dozen eggs:
   - The average cost of a new home:
   - A first-class stamp:
   - A new car:
   - A gallon of gas:
   - A movie ticket:

WHAT KIND OF STUDENT WERE YOU?

"Every father should remember that one day his child will follow his example, not his advice." — Charles Kettering

1. What did you like and dislike about school?

   _____

   _____

   _____

   _____

2. What kind of grades did you get?

   _____

   _____

3. What were your favorite and least favorite subjects?

   _____

   _____

4. What was your relationship with your parents like during your high school years?

   _____

   _____

   _____

   _____

WHAT KIND OF STUDENT WERE YOU?

"Parenthood remains the single greatest preserve
of the amateur." — Alvin Toffler

5. Did you play any sports?

_____

_____

6. What were the school activities that you took part in?

_____

_____

_____

7. Is there a teacher or coach that had a significant
   impact on you? What was their biggest influence?

_____

_____

_____

_____

_____

_____

_____

_____

WHAT KIND OF STUDENT WERE YOU?

"We don't stop going to school when we graduate."
— Carol Burnett

8. What were a few of your favorite songs from your high school years?

_____

_____

_____

_____

_____

9. What would you have done differently in school if you knew then what you know now?

_____

_____

_____

_____

_____

_____

_____

_____

_____

WHAT KIND OF STUDENT WERE YOU?

"Education is what remains after one has forgotten what one has learned in school." — Albert Einstein

10. Write about a favorite memory from your high school years.

_____

_____

_____

_____

_____

_____

_____

_____

_____

_____

_____

_____

_____

_____

_____

_____

_____

DAD TRIVIA

"It is easier to build strong children than to repair broken men." — Frederick Douglass

1. What is your favorite flavor of ice cream?

   _____

2. How do you like your coffee?

   _____

3. How do you like your eggs cooked?

   _____

4. If money were not a concern, where would you want to live?

   _____

   _____

5. Do you still have your tonsils?

   _____

6. What is your shoe size?

   _____

7. How old were you when you started to walk?

   _____

8. Do you have any allergies?

   _____

   _____

   _____

DAD TRIVIA

"Regardless of the personal relationship you have with your own father, you have to aim to be better." — Kirsten Watson

9. What is the eye color of each of your kids?

_____

_____

_____

_____

_____

10. What superpower would you pick for yourself?

_____

_____

11. What would you pick as your last meal?

_____

_____

_____

_____

_____

12. Preference: cook or clean?

_____

13. Were you a Boy Scout?

_____

YOUR PARENTS

"Blessed indeed is the man who hears many gentle voices
call him father." — Lydia Maria Child

1. Where was your mother born and where did she grow up?

_____

_____

_____

_____

2. What three words would you use to describe her?

_____

_____

_____

3. In what ways are you most like your mother?

_____

_____

_____

_____

_____

_____

_____

YOUR PARENTS

"Life doesn't come with an instruction book...that's why
we have fathers." — H. Jackson Browne

4. Where was your father born and where did he grow
   up?

   _____

   _____

   _____

   _____

5. What three words would you use to describe him?

   _____

   _____

   _____

6. In what ways are you like your father?

   _____

   _____

   _____

   _____

   _____

   _____

   _____

YOUR PARENTS

"It kills you to see them grow up. But I guess it would kill you
quicker if they didn't." — Barbara Kingsolver

7. How did your parents meet?

_____

_____

_____

_____

_____

8. Describe your parent's relationship.

_____

_____

_____

_____

_____

_____

9. Did either of them have any unique talents?

_____

_____

_____

_____

YOUR PARENTS

"A father is a man who expects his children to be as
good as he meant to be." — Carol Coats

10. Do we have any family traditions that come from your
parents or grandparents?

_____

_____

_____

_____

11. What were your parent's occupations?

_____

_____

_____

12. What other individuals had a major role in helping
you grow up? What were their biggest influences?

_____

_____

_____

_____

_____

_____

_____

MEMORIES

"Memory is a way of holding on to the things you love, the things you are, the things you never want to lose." — Unknown

What is a favorite memory of your Mother?

_____

_____

_____

_____

_____

_____

_____

_____

_____

_____

_____

_____

_____

_____

_____

_____

_____

_____

MEMORIES

"We don't remember days, we remember moments."
— Unknown

What is a favorite memory of your Father?

_____

_____

_____

_____

_____

_____

_____

_____

_____

_____

_____

_____

_____

_____

_____

_____

_____

_____

BECOMING A DAD

"Dads are ordinary men turned by love into heroes, adventurers, story-tellers, and singers of song." — Pam Brown

1. How old were you when you first became a father?

   _____

2. Who was the first person you told that you were going to be a dad?

   _____

   _____

   _____

3. Is there a specific song you would sing or play to your kids when they were little?

   _____

   _____

4. What is the biggest difference in how kids are raised today than when you were a kid?

   _____

   _____

   _____

   _____

   _____

BECOMING A DAD

"My father used to play with my brother and me in the yard.
Mother would come out and say, 'You're tearing up the grass.'
'We're not raising grass,' Dad would reply. 'We're raising boys.'"
— Harmon Killebrew

5. What are the ways you would change about how your kids were raised?

_____

_____

_____

_____

_____

_____

6. Knowing what you know now, what advice would you give yourself as a new father?

_____

_____

_____

_____

_____

_____

BECOMING A DAD

"There is no greater name for a leader than mother or father.
There is no leadership more important than parenthood."
— Sheri L. Dew

7. What is the best and hardest parts about being a father?

_____

_____

_____

_____

_____

_____

_____

_____

_____

_____

_____

_____

_____

_____

_____

_____

BECOMING A DAD

"Being a great father is like shaving. No matter how good you shaved today, you have to do it again tomorrow."
— Reed Markham

8. Write about a favorite memory of being a father.

_____

_____

_____

_____

_____

_____

_____

_____

_____

_____

_____

_____

_____

_____

_____

_____

_____

_____

"How pleasant
it is for
a father to sit
at his child's board.
It is like an aged man
reclining
under the shadow
of an oak which he
has planted."
-Walter Scott

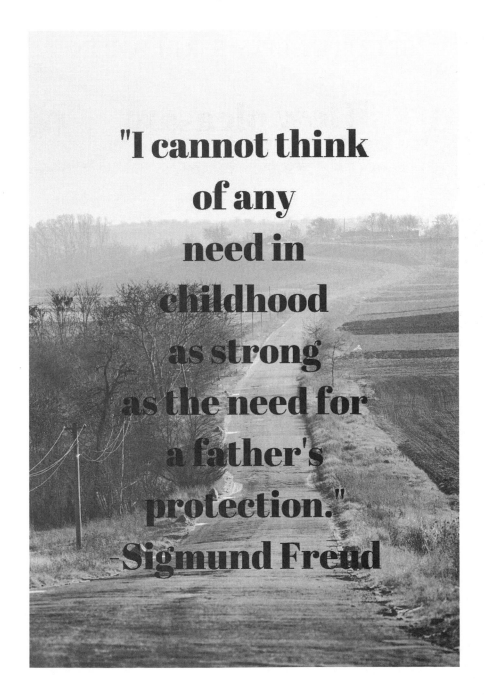

"I cannot think of any need in childhood as strong as the need for a father's protection." -Sigmund Freud

SPIRITUALITY & RELIGION

"A good father is one of the most unsung, unpraised, unnoticed,
and yet one of the most valuable assets in our society."
— Billy Graham

1. Were your parents religious when you were growing up?

   _____

2. How did your parents express their spiritual beliefs?

   _____

   _____

   _____

   _____

3. What role does religion have in your life?

   _____

   _____

   _____

4. Do you believe in miracles? Have you experienced one?

   _____

   _____

   _____

SPIRITUALITY & RELIGION

"The quality of a father can be seen in the goals, dreams and aspirations he sets not only for himself, but for his family." — Reed Markham

5. What do you have faith in?

_____

_____

_____

_____

_____

6. Do you pray? If yes, how often and to whom do you pray?

_____

_____

_____

7. How have your religious beliefs and practices changed over the course of your life?

_____

_____

_____

_____

_____

_____

SPIRITUALITY & RELIGION

"Lookin' back all I can say about all the things he did for me is I
hope I'm at least half the dad that he didn't have to be."
— Brad Paisley

8. What is your current religious or spiritual practice?

_____

_____

_____

_____

_____

_____

_____

_____

9. Which do you think has the most impact on our lives:
fate or free will? Why do you feel this way?

_____

_____

_____

_____

_____

_____

_____

_____

SPIRITUALITY & RELIGION

"Do or Do Not. There is no Try." — Yoda

10. What do you think is the purpose of life?

_____

_____

_____

_____

_____

_____

_____

11. What do you do in moments when times are challenging, and you need inner strength?

_____

_____

_____

_____

_____

_____

_____

_____

WORK & CAREER

"Great teamwork is the only way we create the breakthroughs that define our careers" — Pat Riley

1. When you were a kid, what did you want to be when you grew up?

   _____

   _____

2. What was your first job?

   _____

   _____

3. How many jobs have you had during your lifetime? List a few of your favorites.

   _____

   _____

   _____

   _____

4. What are the favorite and least favorite jobs you have had?

   _____

   _____

   _____

WORK & CAREER
"I'm a great believer in luck, and I find the harder I work,
the more I have of it." — Thomas Jefferson

5. Have you ever wanted to have your own business? If
yes, what kind of business would it be?

_____

_____

_____

6. What are three jobs you would never want to have?

_____

_____

_____

7. Is there a job or profession your parents wanted you
to pursue? If yes, what was it?

_____

_____

_____

8. If you could do any profession, what would it be?

_____

_____

_____

_____

DAD TRIVIA

"A father is only capable of giving what he has, and what he
knows. A good father gives all of himself that is good."
— Vincent Carrella

1. Do you read your horoscope?

    _____

2. What motivates you?

    _____

    _____

    _____

    _____

3. What is your biggest big pet peeve?

    _____

4. Do you ever buy lottery tickets?

    _____

5. What is your favorite season of the year?

    _____

6. If you could do any one thing for a day, what would it
    be?

    _____

    _____

    _____

7. Have you ever fired a gun?

    _____

DAD TRIVIA

"Fatherhood is the best thing that could happen to me, and I'm
just glad I can share my voice." — Dwyane Wade

8. Who is your hero? Why?

_____

_____

_____

_____

_____

9. If you could only eat three things for the next year,
with no harm to your health, what would they be?

_____

_____

_____

10. What can you do better than anyone else in the
family?

_____

_____

_____

11. What were the names of your childhood pets?

_____

_____

_____

_____

LOVE & ROMANCE

"If I had a flower for every time, I thought of you...I could walk
through my garden forever." — Alfred Tennyson

1. What was the biggest crush you had when you were in
high school?

_____

_____

_____

2. What age were you when you had your first date?

_____

3. Who was it with and what did you do?

_____

_____

_____

_____

_____

4. How old were you when you had your first kiss?

_____

5. Do you believe in love at first sight?

_____

LOVE & ROMANCE
"We love the things we love for what they are." — Robert Frost

6. Do you believe in soul mates?

_____

7. Have you ever written someone a love poem or song?

_____

8. If yes, write a few lines that you may remember.

_____

_____

_____

_____

9. What is your most romantic memory?

_____

_____

_____

_____

_____

_____

LOVE & ROMANCE

"You know you're in love when you can't fall asleep because reality is finally better than your dreams." — Dr. Seuss

10. What is your opinion of online dating?

_____

_____

_____

11. What are the most important qualities of a successful relationship?

_____

_____

_____

_____

_____

12. What is the biggest way relationships have changed over the years?

_____

_____

_____

_____

_____

LOVE & ROMANCE

"It is not a lack of love, but a lack of friendship that makes unhappy marriages." — Friedrich Nietzsche

13. Write about a time you experienced a broken heart. How did you get over it?

_____

_____

_____

_____

_____

_____

_____

_____

_____

_____

_____

_____

_____

_____

_____

_____

_____

_____

TRAVEL
"Once a year, go someplace you've never been before."
— Dali Lama

1. Do you have a valid passport?

   _____

2. What is your fantasy vacation?

   _____

   _____

   _____

3. Are you a light or heavy packer?

   _____

4. What is the one thing from home you always bring
   with you on a trip?

   _____

   _____

5. When traveling, do you stick to familiar foods or do
   you look for places where the locals eat?

   _____

   _____

   _____

TRAVEL

"A mind that is stretched by a new experience can never go back to its old dimensions." — Oliver Wendell Holmes

6. What is your favorite travel memory?

_____

_____

_____

_____

_____

_____

_____

_____

7. Write about a travel memory from when you were a kid.

_____

_____

_____

_____

_____

_____

_____

TRAVEL BUCKET LIST
"Life is short, and the world is wide." — Unknown

List the top 10 places you would visit if money and time were no concern. Write about why for each choice.

1. _____

_____

2. _____

_____

3. _____

_____

4. _____

_____

5. _____

_____

TRAVEL BUCKET LIST

"Travel makes one modest, you see what a tiny place you occupy in the world." — Gustave Flaubert

Continued

6. _____

_____

7. _____

_____

8. _____

_____

9. _____

_____

10. _____

_____

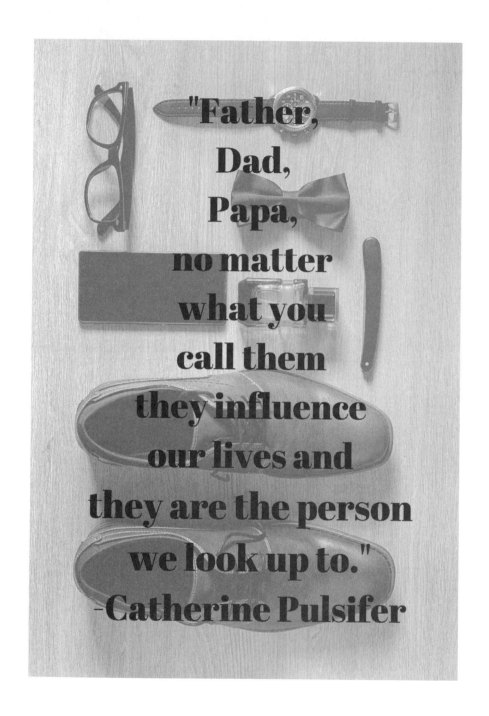

"Father, Dad, Papa, no matter what you call them they influence our lives and they are the person we look up to." -Catherine Pulsifer

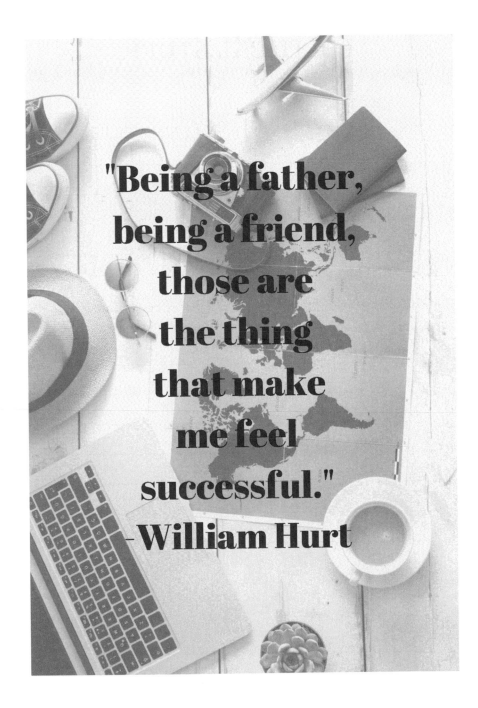

"Being a father, being a friend, those are the thing that make me feel successful." - William Hurt

POLITICAL STUFF

"What you teach your children, you also teach their children."
— Unknown

1. How old were you when you voted for the first time?

   _____

2. When was the last time you voted?

   _____

3. How have your political opinions changed over the years?

   _____

   _____

   _____

   _____

   _____

   _____

   _____

4. What do you think are the three most serious issues facing our country?

   _____

   _____

   _____

POLITICAL STUFF

"Children have never been very good at listening to their elders,
but they have never failed to imitate them." — James Baldwin

5. Have you ever participated in a march or boycott? If
no, what issue could motivate you to join?

_____

_____

_____

6. Who in your family would you guess votes differently
than you?

_____

_____

_____

7. Who is your favorite political or historical figure?
Why do you admire them?

_____

_____

_____

_____

_____

POLITICAL STUFF

"Politics, it seems to me, has been concerned with right or left instead of right or wrong." — Richard Armour

8. What are the positive and negative impacts your generation has had on the country and the world?

_____

_____

_____

_____

_____

_____

_____

9. Discuss the ways you agree and disagree with the political choices of your children's generation.

_____

_____

_____

_____

_____

_____

POLITICAL STUFF
"In politics stupidity is not a handicap."
— Napoleon Bonaparte

10. Who is the best president of your lifetime?

_____

11. If you woke up tomorrow and found yourself in charge of the entire country, what are the first five things would you enact or change?

One:

_____

_____

Two:

_____

_____

Three:

_____

_____

Four:

_____

_____

Five:

_____

_____

SECRETS

"Before I got married, I had six theories about raising children; now, I have six children and no theories." — John Wilmot

1. Is there ever a time when it is okay to tell a lie? What was a time when you felt the need to tell one?

   _____

   _____

   _____

   _____

2. Have you ever read someone else's private mail, email, diary, or journal? If yes, what was the situation?

   _____

   _____

   _____

   _____

3. What is your worst habit? What are you doing to try and change it?

   _____

   _____

   _____

   _____

SECRETS

"The older I get, the smarter my father seems to get."
— Tim Russert

4. Have you ever secretly looked through someone's medicine cabinet?

_____

5. Did you ever skip school?

_____

6. If yes, what did you do during the time you should have been in class?

_____

_____

_____

7. Write about a major regret from your past.

_____

_____

_____

_____

_____

_____

LET'S TALK ABOUT YOUR KIDS
"One father is more than a hundred schoolmasters."
— George Herbert

1. What would your kids names be if they had been born the opposite gender?

   _____

   _____

   _____

   _____

2. Who did your children most look like when they were babies?

   _____

   _____

   _____

   _____

   _____

3. What were your kids' first words?

   _____

   _____

   _____

   _____

   _____

LET'S TALK ABOUT YOUR KIDS

"The most important thing a father can do for his children is to
love their mother." — Theodore Hesburgh

4. How old were they when they took their first step?

_____

_____

_____

_____

5. How many of your children were planned and how
   many were surprises?

_____

_____

6. Is there a specific book you remember reading to
   your kids?

_____

_____

7. When your kids were babies, what trick did you use to
   calm them when they were upset?

_____

_____

_____

LET'S TALK ABOUT YOUR KIDS
"Adults are just outdated children." — Dr. Seuss

8. What is your first memory of each of your children?

_____

_____

_____

_____

_____

_____

_____

_____

_____

_____

_____

_____

_____

_____

_____

_____

LET'S TALK ABOUT YOUR KIDS

"Children are a poor man's riches." — English Proverb

9. In what ways are your kids like you and how are they different?

_____

_____

_____

_____

_____

_____

_____

_____

_____

_____

_____

_____

_____

_____

_____

DAD TRIVIA

"I have found the best way to give advice to your children is to find out what they want and then advise them to do it."
— Harry S. Truman

1. What would be the title of your autobiography?

   _____

   _____

   _____

2. Do you think you could still pass the written portion of the driver's test without studying?

   _____

3. What is your favorite line from a movie?

   _____

   _____

   _____

   _____

4. Do you believe in life on other planets?

   _____

   _____

5. If you were forced to sing karaoke, what song would you pick to perform?

   _____

   _____

   _____

   _____

DAD TRIVIA

"When I was a kid, my parents moved a lot,
but I always found them."
— Rodney Dangerfield

6. What is your favorite color?

_____

7. What is the first movie you can remember seeing?

_____

_____

8. Who was your role model growing up? What impact did they have on you?

_____

_____

_____

_____

_____

_____

_____

9. When was the last time a movie or something on television made you cry? What was it?

_____

_____

_____

SPORTS MEMORIES

"Anyone can be a father, but it takes someone
special to be a dad." — Wade Boggs

1. When you were a kid, did you ever think about being a professional athlete? Which sport?

_____

_____

2. Growing up, what was your favorite sport? Did you have a favorite team?

_____

_____

3. Who is your favorite player of all time in any sport?

_____

_____

_____

4. If money and time was no object, what sporting event do you most want to attend?

_____

_____

_____

_____

SPORTS MEMORIES

"My father gave me the greatest gift anyone could give another
person, he believed in me." — Jim Valvano

5. What was the first professional sporting event you
    attended in person?

    _____

    _____

6. What was the most crushing defeat you experienced
    playing or watching a sporting event?

    _____

    _____

    _____

7. Is there a sporting event you saw as a kid that you
    still vividly remember?

    _____

    _____

    _____

    _____

8. What is your favorite sports movie?

    _____

    _____

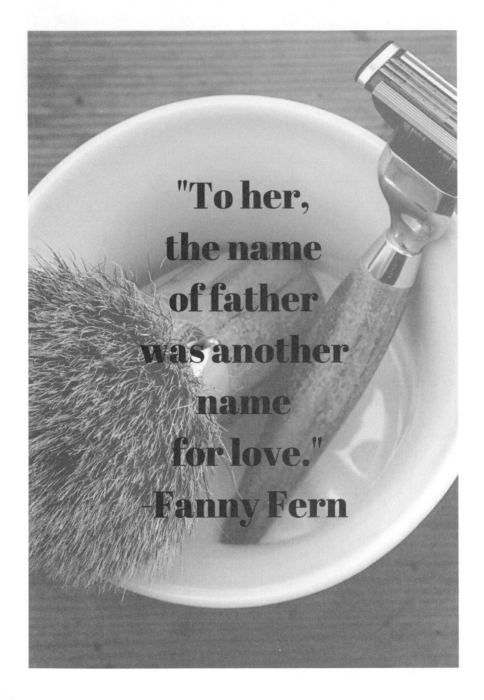

"To her, the name of father was another name for love." -Fanny Fern

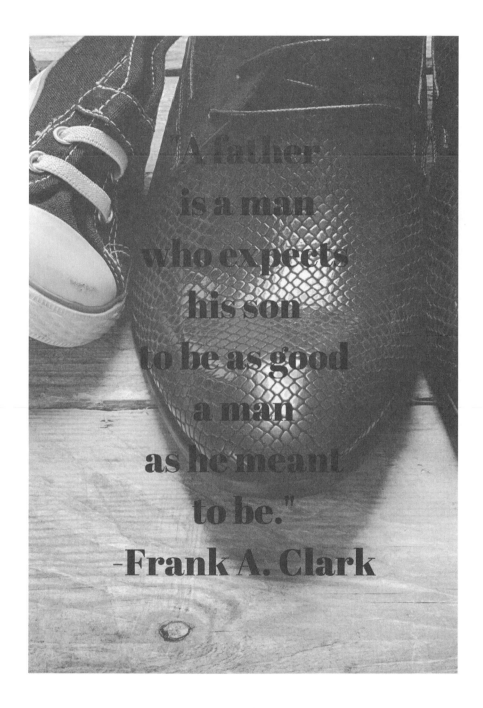

"A father is a man who expects his son to be as good a man as he meant to be."
-Frank A. Clark

MOVIES, MUSIC, TELEVISION, & BOOKS

"The soul is healed by being with children."
— Fyodor Dostoevsky

1. What movie do you think you have watched the greatest number of times?

   _____

   _____

2. What is a movie you can remember loving when you were a kid?

   _____

   _____

   _____

3. Who would you cast to play yourself in the movie of your life? How about the rest of your family?

   _____

   _____

   _____

   _____

   _____

   _____

   _____

MOVIES, MUSIC, TELEVISION, & BOOKS

"Children must be taught how to think, not what to think."
— Margaret Mead

4. What are your favorite genres of music?

_____

_____

_____

_____

5. Which decades had the best music?

_____

_____

_____

6. What is the first record, album, cassette, or tape you remember buying?

_____

_____

7. What song do you like today that would make your younger self cringe?

_____

_____

MOVIES, MUSIC, TELEVISION, & BOOKS

"Children are the living messages we send to a time
we will not see. — John F. Kennedy

8. What was the first concert you attended? What year
was it?

_____

_____

9. How has your taste in music changed over the years?

_____

_____

_____

_____

_____

10. What is the first song you can remember loving?

_____

_____

11. If you had to pick a theme song for your life, what
song would you pick??

_____

_____

MOVIES, MUSIC, TELEVISION, & BOOKS

"Children see magic because they look for it."
— Christopher Moore

12. What television show from the past do you wish was still on the air?

_____

_____

13. If you could be on any television show or movie, past or present, which one would you pick?

_____

_____

14. What is a favorite book from your childhood or teen years?

_____

_____

15. What book or books have positively impacted the way you think, work, or live your life?

_____

_____

_____

_____

TOP TEN MOVIES
"Children need models rather than critics."— Joseph Joubert

List Your Ten Most Favorite Movies:

1. _____

_____

2. _____

_____

3. _____

_____

4. _____

_____

5. _____

_____

6. _____

_____

7. _____

_____

8. _____

_____

9. _____

_____

10. _____

TOP TEN SONGS

"Daddies don't just love their children every now and then, it's a love without end." — George Straight

List Your Ten Most Favorite Songs:

1. _____

_____

2. _____

_____

3. _____

_____

4. _____

_____

5. _____

_____

6. _____

_____

7. _____

_____

8. _____

_____

9. _____

_____

10. _____

DAD TRIVIA

"It is not flesh and blood, but heart which makes us
fathers and sons." — Friedrich von Schiller

1. How many speeding tickets have you received?

   _____

2. What is your favorite holiday?

   _____

3. If you could have dinner with any five people who
   have ever lived, who would you pick?

   _____

   _____

   _____

   _____

   _____

   _____

4. What bones have you broken?

   _____

   _____

   _____

   _____

5. What is your dream car?

   _____

   _____

DAD TRIVIA
"My Dad was what defined being a man was."
— Author Unknown

6. What accomplishment are you most proud of yourself for achieving?

_____

_____

_____

_____

_____

7. Is there anything in your family's medical history that your kids should know about?

_____

_____

_____

_____

_____

8. What is your favorite thing about yourself?

_____

_____

_____

_____

"You don't raise heroes, you raise sons. And if you treat them like sons, they'll turn out to be heroes, even if it's just in your own eyes."
- Walter M. Schirra, Sr.

"The nature of
impending
fatherhood
is that you
are doing something
that you're
unqualified to do, and
then you become
qualified
while doing it"
-John Greene

ADVICE

"Sometimes the poorest man leaves his children
the richest inheritance." — Ruth E. Renkel

What was the best advice your mother gave you?

_____

_____

_____

_____

_____

_____

What was the best advice your father gave you?

_____

_____

_____

_____

_____

_____

ADVICE

"Children are likely to live up to what you believe of them."
— Lady Bird Johnson

Based upon what you have learned and what you have experienced, what is the one key piece of advice you would give your children?

_____

_____

_____

_____

_____

_____

_____

_____

_____

_____

_____

_____

_____

_____

_____

_____

QUESTIONS

"When you have brought up kids, there are memories you store
directly in your tear ducts." — Robert Brault

What questions have you always wanted to ask your
parents?

_____

_____

_____

_____

_____

_____

What questions would you like your kids to ask you?

_____

_____

_____

_____

_____

_____

QUESTIONS

"Children are not only innocent and curious but also optimistic and joyful and essentially happy. They are, in short, everything adults wish they could be." — Carolyn Haywood

How would you like to be remembered by your family and friends?

_____

_____

_____

_____

_____

_____

_____

_____

_____

_____

_____

_____

_____

_____

_____

NOTES TO THOSE I LOVE

"The best inheritance a parent can give his children is a few minutes of his time each day." — Orlando Aloysius Battista

This is space for you to write notes to your family.

_____

_____

_____

_____

_____

_____

_____

_____

_____

_____

_____

_____

_____

_____

_____

_____

_____

NOTES TO THOSE I LOVE

"Don't worry that children never listen to you; worry that they are always watching you." — Robert Fulghum

This is space for you to write notes to your family.

_____

_____

_____

_____

_____

_____

_____

_____

_____

_____

_____

_____

_____

_____

_____

_____

NOTES TO THOSE I LOVE

"Children are like wet cement: whatever falls on them makes an impression." — Haim Ginott

This is space for you to write notes to your family.

_____

_____

_____

_____

_____

_____

_____

_____

_____

_____

_____

_____

_____

_____

_____

NOTES TO THOSE I LOVE

"You have to love your children unselfishly. That is hard. But it is the only way." — Barbara Bush

This is space for you to write notes to your family.

_____

_____

_____

_____

_____

_____

_____

_____

_____

_____

_____

_____

_____

_____

_____

_____

NOTES TO THOSE I LOVE

"The best way to make children good is to make them happy."
— Oscar Wilde

This is space for you to write notes to your family.

_____

_____

_____

_____

_____

_____

_____

_____

_____

_____

_____

_____

_____

_____

_____

_____

NOTES TO THOSE I LOVE

"The greatest gifts you can give your children are the roots of responsibility and the wings of independence." — Denis Waitley

This is space for you to write notes to your family.

_____

_____

_____

_____

_____

_____

_____

_____

_____

_____

_____

_____

_____

_____

_____

_____

_____

MOVIES ABOUT DADS
"A father is the one friend upon whom we can always rely."
— Emile Gaboriau

- The Kid (1921)
- The Champ (1931)
- It's a Wonderful Life (1946)
- Bicycle Thieves (1948)
- Father of the Bride (1950)
- Father's Little Dividend (1951)
- To Kill a Mockingbird (1962)
- Yours, Mine, and Ours (1968)
- The Godfather (1972)
- Paper Moon (1973)
- Kramer vs. Kramer (1979)
- The Great Santini (1979)
- The Empire Strikes Back (1980)
- Mr. Mom (1983)
- National Lampoon's Vacation (1983)
- National Lampoon's European Vacation (1985)
- Three Men and a Baby (1987)
- Die Hard (1988)
- Parenthood (1989)
- Field of Dreams (1989)

MORE MOVIES ABOUT DADS

"A father is someone you look up to no matter
how tall you grow." — Unknown

- Dad (1989)

- National Lampoon's Christmas Vacation (1989)

- Indiana Jones and the Last Crusade (1989)

- Father of the Bride (1991)

- Mrs. Doubtfire (1993)

- My Life (1993)

- The Lion King (1994)

- Father of the Bride (1995)

- Man of the House (1995)

- Fly Away Home (1996)

- Jingle All the Way (1996)

- Life is Beautiful (1997)

- Father's Day (1997)

- He Got Game (1998)

- Big Daddy (1999)

- The Family Man (2000)

- Frequency (2000)

- The Royal Tenenbaums (2001)

- I Am Sam (2001)

- Signs (2002)

MORE MOVIES ABOUT DADS

"Children are the hands by which we take hold of heaven."
— Henry Ward Beecher

- John Q (2002)
- Daddy Day Care (2003)
- Big Fish (2003)
- Elf (2003)
- Finding Nemo (2003)
- Cheaper by the Dozen (2003)
- The Incredibles (2004)
- Jersey Girl (2004)
- The Life Aquatic with Steve Zissou (2004)
- Raising Helen (2004)
- Yours, Mine, & Ours (2005)
- The Pursuit of Happiness (2006)
- The Game Plan (2007)
- Daddy's Little Girls (2007)
- Juno (2007)
- Are We Done Yet? (2007)
- Taken (2008)
- Definitely, Maybe (2008)
- Beginners (2010)
- The Spy Next Door (2010)

MORE MOVIES ABOUT DADS

"When a father gives to his son, both laugh. When a son gives to his father, both cry." — William Shakespeare

- Somewhere (2010)

- The Switch (2010)

- Tron: Legacy (2010)

- The Tree of Life (2011)

- The Descendants (2011)

- We Bought a Zoo (2011)

- Trouble with the Curve (2012)

- Nebraska (2013)

- Instructions Not Included (2013)

- Chef (2014)

- Interstellar (2014)

- Blended (2014)

- Daddy's Home (2015)

- Fathers and Daughters (2015)

- Daddy's Home 2 (2017)

- Of Fathers and Sons (2017)

- Incredibles 2 (2018)

- Beautiful Boy (2018)

- Instant Family (2018)

- The Secret Garden (2020)

SONGS ABOUT DADS

"When my son looks up to me and breaks into his toothless smile, my eyes fill up and I know that having him is the best thing I will ever do." — Dan Greenberg

- Perry Como, "Papa Loves Mambo" (1954)

- The Temptations, "My Girl" (1965)

- Johnny Cash, "A Boy Named Sue" (1969)

- Leon Thomas, "Song for My Father" (1969)

- Cat Stevens, "Father & Son" (1970)

- Loggins and Messina "Danny's Song" (1971)

- David Bowie, "Kooks" (1971)

- Neil Young, "Old Man" (1971)

- Bobby Goldsboro, "Watching Scotty Grow" (1971)

- Temptations, "Papa Was a Rollin' Stone" (1972)

- Neil Diamond, "Dear Father" (1973)

- Harry Chapin, "Cat's in the Cradle" (1974)

- Queen, "Father to Son" (1974)

- James Brown, "Papa Don't Take No Mess (1974)

- Stevie Wonder, "Isn't She Lovely" (1976)

- Bob Dylan, "Forever Young" (1976)

- John Lennon, "Beautiful Boy (Darling Boy)" (1980)

- Bruce Springsteen, "Independence Day" (1980)

- Dan Fogelberg, "The Leader of the Band" (1981)

- Bruce Springsteen, "My Father's House" (1982)

MORE SONGS ABOUT DADS

"We spend the first year of a child's life teaching it to walk and talk and the rest of its life to shut up and sit down. There's something wrong there." — Neil deGrasse Tyson

- Talking Heads, "Up All Night" (1985)

- Holly Dunn, "Daddy's Hands" (1986)

- Madonna, "Papa Don't Preach" (1986)

- Conway Twitty, "That's My Job" (1987)

- Jane's Addictions, "Had a Dad" (1988)

- Mike + The Mechanics, "The Living Years" (1988)

- Bette Midler, "Wind Beneath My Wings" (1988)

- Madonna, "Oh Father" (1989)

- Phil Collins, "Father to Son" (1989)

- George Strait, "Love Without End, Amen (1990)

- Natalie Cole w/Nat King Cole "Unforgettable" (1991)

- Reba McEntire, "The Greatest Man I Never Knew" (1991)

- Billy Joel, "Lullaby (Good Night My Angel)" (1993)

- 2Pac, "Papa's Song" (1994)

- George Strait, "The Best Day" (1994)

- Allman Brothers Band, "Soulshine" (1994)

- Will Smith, "Just the Two of Us" (1997)

- Bob Carlisle, "Butterfly Kisses" (1997)

- Eric Clapton, "My Father's Eyes" (1998)

MORE SONGS ABOUT DADS

"Each day of our lives we make deposits in the memory banks of our children." — Charles R. Swindoll

- Brad Paisley, "He Didn't Have to Be" (1999)

- 2Pac, "To My Unborn Child" (2001)

- Lonestar, "I'm Already There" (2001)

- Keith Urban, "Song for Dad" (2002)

- Alan Jackson, "Drive (For Daddy Gene)" (2002)

- Michael Bublé, "Daddy's Little Girl" (2002)

- Luther Vandross, "Dance with My Father" (2003)

- Josh Groban, "You Lift Me Up" (2003)

- John Mayer, "Daughters" (2003)

- Beyoncé, "Daddy" (2003)

- Yellowcard, "Life of a Salesman" (2003)

- Keith Urban, "There Goes My Life" (2004)

- U2, "Sometimes You Can't Make It on Your Own"

- The Game, "Like Father, Like Son" (2005)

- Depeche Mode, "Precious" (2005)

- Neil Young, "Here for You" (2005)

- Paul Simon, "Father and Daughter" (2006)

- Rascal Flatts, "My Wish" (2006)

- Tim McGraw, "My Little Girl" (2006)

- Billy Ray Cyrus & Miley Cyrus, "I Learned from You

MORE SONGS ABOUT DADS

"Old as she was, she still missed her daddy sometimes."
— Gloria Naylor

- Loudon Wainwright, "Daughter" (2007)

- Brad Paisley, "Letter to Me" (2007)

- Darius Rucker, "It Won't Be Like This for Long" (2008)

- Traci Adkins, "You're Gonna Miss This" (2009)

- Taylor Swift, "The Best Day" (2009)

- Animal Collective, "My Girls" (2009)

- Jon Barker, "Thank You for Being My Dad" (2010)

- Clark Richard, "Red Robin" (2010)

- Tracie Adkins, "Just Fishin" (2011)

- Jay Z, "Glory" (2012)

- Regina Carter, "Daddy's Little Girl" (2013)

- Craig Cardiff, "Father Daughter Dance" (2013)

- Robbie Williams, "Go Gentle" (2013)

- Kanye West w/Paul McCartney, "Only One" (2014)

- David Ryan Harris, "I Can't Wait to Meet You" (2014)

- Zac Brown Band, "I'll Be Your Man" (2014)

- Beyoncé w/The Chicks, "Daddy Lessons" (2016)

- John Legend, "Right by You (For Luna)" (2016)

- Zac Brown Band, "My Old Man" (2017)

About This Book

In today's world, the rush and responsibilities too often nudge away time with our family and friends.

We do our best, but often find ourselves stretched thin and lack time to focus on the people in our lives.

Our kids become unsure of when we are available and turn to us less and less. Our conversations with them become infrequent and understanding each other gets harder and harder.

When we do talk, it ends up being often discipline instead of guidance.

The purpose of "Dad, I Want to Hear Your Story" is to create conversations that reconnect us to ourselves and our families. Sharing our life experiences helps others understand who we are and why we are the way we are.

Our families hear our hopes and needs, and they see the roots of our feelings and fears. We get better at pausing and talking and our kids become more comfortable coming to us.

Fathering a child takes a moment but being a father takes a lifetime. It is relentlessly hard, requires our full investment and involvement. It is also the best and most important thing any of us will ever do.

About the Author

Jeffrey Mason has spent twenty-plus years working with individuals, couples, and organizations helping them to create change, achieve goals, and strengthen their relationships.

He begins with the understanding that being human is hard and is committed to helping others understand that forgiveness is the greatest gift we can give others and ourselves.

He wants all of to remember that while we have eternity, we do not have forever.

Jeffrey would be grateful if you would help people find his books by leaving a review on Amazon. Your feedback helps him get better at this thing he loves.

You can contact him at hello@jeffreymason.com. He would love to hear from you.

The Hear Your Story Line of Books

At **Hear Your Story**, we have created a line of books focused on giving each of us a place to tell the unique story of who we are, where we have been, and where we are going.

Sharing and hearing the stories of the people in our lives creates communication, closeness, understanding, and the cement of a forever bond.

- Dad, I Want to Hear Your Story; A Father's Guided Journal to Share His Life & His Love

- Mom, I Want to Hear Your Story; A Mother's Guided Journal to Share Her Life & Her Love

- You Chose to Be My Dad; I Want to Hear Your Story: A Guided Journal for Stepdads to Share Their Life Story

- Life Gave Me You; I Want to Hear Your Story: A Guided Journal for Stepmothers to Share Their Life Story

The Hear Your Story Line of Books

- Grandmother, I Want to Hear Your Story: A Grandmother's Guided Journal to Share Her Life and Her Love

- Grandfather, I Want to Hear Your Story: A Grandfather's Guided Journal to Share His Life and His Love

- Dad Notes: Dad, I Wrote This Book for You

- Mom Notes: I Wrote This Book About the Best Mother Ever

- Because I Love You: The Couple's Bucket List That Builds Your Relationship

- Love Notes: I Wrote This Book About You

- Our Story: A Couple's Guided Journal

- You, Me, and Us: 229 Fun Relationship Questions to Ask Your Guy or Girl

- Papá, quiero oír tu historia: El diario guiado de un padre Para compartir su vida y su amor

Available at Amazon and all Bookstores

"Anyone who tells you fatherhood is the greatest thing that can happen to you, they are understating it."
-Mike Myers